Seven Brave Women

A Midwife Looks at the Birth of the Church

SALLY LOMBARDO

WESTBOW
PRESS®
A DIVISION OF THOMAS NELSON
& ZONDERVAN

WestBow Press books may be ordered through booksellers or by contacting:

WestBow Press
A Division of Thomas Nelson & Zondervan
1663 Liberty Drive
Bloomington, IN 47403
www.westbowpress.com
844-714-3454

Interior Image Credit:
Uncut Mountain Supply
orthodoxdeaconess.org

ISBN: 978-1-6642-1370-8 (sc)
ISBN: 978-1-6642-1371-5 (e)

Library of Congress Control Number: 2020923393

Print information available on the last page.

WestBow Press rev. date: 03/15/2021

Introduction

Seven relatively unknown women in the early church setting—Mary Magdalene, Priscilla, Lydia, Chloe, Phoebe, Nympha, and Junia—worked to change history for the Christian world. With courage, they created underground churches, supported apostles, and taught the gospel. Few texts examine the history of these brave women and compare them to women of today. In the pages that follow, I describe Mary Magdalene's unique role as a disciple, a few of the other "Mary" followers, and explain the roles of the women mentioned by Paul in Acts, 1 Corinthians, and Romans 16. Apocryphal stories also shed light on this piece of history and cite the unique place of the home church during a time of persecution and fear. I will provide detailed accounts of the seven women who brought significant change to first-century society. My purpose is to examine their lives and daring choices within the context, culture, and community in which each may have lived.

The book of Acts is the story of how the church was born amid courage and triumph and pain. Jesus's death and resurrection erupted into a movement that would launch the Christian era, and followers would band together in a new community they called *ekklesia*— a church. We have become the continuation of that earth-shattering birth, keepers of the covenant faith. In a well-loved book entitled *The Pastor,* the author explains that the first Christians evolved into a church as they participated in the memory, recorded prayers, and beloved deeds of Jesus Christ. Immersing themselves in these rich stories, the Christian communities of the first century came alive and drew others into their unique perspective on shared life (Peterson *The Pastor.* Harper One 2012, 141). Luke, as writer of his own gospel and of Acts, places the two birth stories in parallel form: first, he describes the supernatural birth of Jesus, and next, he depicts the birth of the Christian church as another extraordinary appearance of God. Both are eruptions of new life, and each bears witness to the invasion of the Holy Spirit into the world. The book of Acts continues the story of Jesus by narrating the description of the birth of the church. Launched by the coming of the Holy Spirit, it would be kept safe by clandestine, early Christian fellowships. The Christian community still propels this work forward today.

How can studying the founders of the ancient church help us today? The early church of the Jesus movement was propelled forward by ordinary brave women. Did Jesus call these certain women who birthed, sheltered, and raised His church, and is He calling me to do the same today? It is my hope that studying the early church will help us better understand our own callings and purposes in life, no matter who we are or where we find our lives today. We, too, can face our journeys with courage, just like the women and men who ushered in the church age.

We begin with the metaphor of birth. Is the miracle of human birth, even Mary's birth of Jesus, similar to the miraculous birth of the early church? Using my biblical examples above, we can conclude that author Luke obviously believed there was connection between the two. Through years of being a midwife and mother, I have discovered that searching for how to bring new life in many endeavors brings great reward. Women bring life to others in so many ways. Peeking into the lives of women in the early church can teach us truths that will bear fruit as we serve in our churches today.

In my own experience, I have fond memories of the ocean. Walking on the beach, you can dig your toes into the sand and find treasure just under the surface. Looking for well-formed shells often brought shark's teeth; looking for sea glass often revealed bits of sand dollars, or sometimes the whole. What could I learn by looking at the lives of women in the ancient world, who dealt with disappointment and fear and pain just as I have? My search took years as a teacher, then a midwife, and later as a seminary student. I taught childbirth classes, English classes, and eventually the Bible. Over time, a series of pregnant girls showed up into my life, both in my den and on my doorstep looking for someone to teach them about courage. I taught them all I knew. In a life of mothering four young boys, these girls became the "daughters" God was granting me.

Years later, after my own daughter arrived, I spent four years in seminary learning about the history of the church and important roles that women played in the spread of the Word. I began to connect the young women whose birth experiences I had shared to the women I studied in the Bible, teaching the hopeful stories of women who followed Jesus and of those who joined Paul. Bravely following despite the cost to their own lives, these women acted as midwives to the gospel itself. Biblical narratives reveal unique pathways for women, paths of courageous independent thought without unnecessary striving or demand. In teaching God's Word, I have watched women find remarkable confidence and self-esteem as they step out in faith.

Let us consider these seven women whose courage and passion helped to create the early church. Building on a foundation laid by outliers Mary Magdalene and Mary the mother of James and Joseph, strong women followed, taking the message of Jesus and hurling it forward to the world. Jewish apostle Priscilla formed the underground church at Corinth; Macedonian Lydia heard Paul speak and converted her household; Corinthian Phoebe took the message to Rome. Pauline supporters Nympha in Colossus, Chloe in Corinth, and Junia were trailblazers who fostered churches in their homes. Each of these women moved ancient boundaries, stood up for her beliefs, and in doing so changed the world.

In the following chapters, I explore why one set of brave actions and choices by one individual paved a way for many to see God's truth and believe in the one He sent. In my years of teaching and mentoring, I have known many people who are reluctant to walk the path toward purpose, freedom and joy that God has opened to them because of cultural expectations or fear. Such people miss, therefore, what they are truly called to do. This book is an effort to change that course.

Three Marys Are Transformed

My first childbirth student was a brave young woman named Casey. She was an unwed mother who courageously decided walk the road alone. I watched this young woman enter companionship with me as a somewhat-insecure and apologetic teen, yet over time as we laughed and learned about the skills and strength she would need to give birth naturally, I watched Casey grow from a timid girl to a bold witness for all she wanted to achieve on her own. We studied the Bible together and talked about God's plan for her as she would soon embrace a baby girl. Casey had a wonderful birth. During her labor, she was supported by me, her own mother, and her best friend. She gave birth in confidence and has grown to be a woman of character and influence, teaching her own students and raising her children with wisdom.

In the same way, new Christians in the first century were called despite their fears to be bold witnesses for Christ, not only with their lives but also with their choices. Everyone who shared the message was taught by the founding apostles to be strong apologists and to give the reason for the hope they clung to. This early story of the church equally involved male and female missionaries, according to Paul's own writings. "I commend to you our sister Phoebe, a deacon in the church at Cenchrae," he says in Romans 16:1. "Welcome her in the Lord as one who is worthy of honor"; and "give my greetings to Priscilla and her husband Aquila, my co-workers in the ministry of Christ Jesus" (Romans 16:3). The vital house ministry of both word and deed necessarily included women, states Michael Green in *Evangelism in the Early Church*, and such women had a large role to play in Christianity's advance. "They were a vital and fundamental part of the church's swift success" (Green 2003, 174).

One can trace this elevation of women's roles back to Jesus Himself. Women involved in the spread of the good news of Jesus were dedicated and loyal, as evidenced by frequent mention in the Bible of their unique personalities and contributions. One can examine the detailed accounts of Jesus's close friends Mary and Martha, who both looked to Jesus for wisdom in personal affairs. Their witness and ministry became part of His teaching as an example to many, with Mary herself described as a devoted disciple; "Mary also sat at the Lord's feet and was listening to what He said," writes Luke (Luke 10:39). Such a posture was the description of a committed and practiced follower, a disciple.

Women were among the large band of believers who supported Jesus as He traveled from one town to another, preaching the good news of the kingdom of God. Luke describes these several named followers as "*certain women* who had been healed of evil spirits and infirmities: *Mary, called Magdalene,* from whom seven demons had gone out, Joanna, wife of Herod's steward Chuza, Susanna, and *many others* who provided from their resources" (Luke 8:1–3; emphasis added). Who were these "certain women"—faithful ones who had followed Jesus closely and later joined the male disciples to band together in the upper room? How did they find the courage and strength to meet in secret? An unnamed woman comes boldly to the house of a Pharisee with an alabaster jar. Although the Pharisee rebukes her, she stands "behind Jesus at His feet, weeping and bathing his feet with her hair … anointing them with oil." Later, Jesus will explain to the disciples, "Her sins, which were many, have been forgiven, as she has shown great love" (Luke 7:36–38, 47). John's Gospel indicates that this woman may have been Jesus's devoted friend and follower, Mary of Bethany (John 12:3).

Mary Magdalene reappears frequently in the Gospel accounts. Mark provides the detail that "Saturday evening, when the Sabbath ended, *Mary Magdalene, Mary the Mother the mother of James, and Salome* purchased burial spices to anoint Jesus' body" (Mark 16:1; emphasis added). A day in the Jewish calendar was measured from dawn to dusk. After this third day had ended, Matthew also states that "many women who had followed Jesus from Galilee and ministered to Him were also there watching at the tomb … among them, *Mary Magdalene, Mary mother of James*, and *Mary mother of Zebedee's sons*" (Matthew 27:55–56; emphasis added). These represent several Marys who had taken care of Jesus in His life and were now participating in His death. They had gone to anoint their rabbi and had no idea they would not find Jesus there. Matthew states that Mary Magdalene and other women were looking on from a distance. The writer of John adds that the next morning Mary Magdalene stood outside the tomb weeping then stooped "and looked into the tomb," as if anticipating Jesus to be alive. She saw the two angels in white and heard Jesus calling her name, asking, "Woman, why are you weeping?" (John 20:12). Mary is the one who runs to the disciples in the place where Jesus also came. She is hurried, frightened, and ecstatic. Luke includes Joanna among the others who go "and tell the apostles all the things they had seen" (Luke 24:10). Their words sound like nonsense, but the women are undaunted. At some level, each must have known she was uniquely called to bear good news.

Mary Magdalene is an intriguing woman. Although we know

little about Mary's actual circumstances, we are told she came from the mountainous region of Magdala, near Capernaum on the Galilean sea. Daily life was dry and arduous, filled with carrying and purifying water, and women were scarcely seen in public outside of the company of family and others of their clan. It is likely Mary had become discontent with Jewish restrictions and had ventured out on her own. She may have discovered Jesus and His disciples at Gennesaret, where He orchestrated the feeding of the multitudes. Traveling with other women to the lake and village on daily routine chores, she may have heard Jesus teaching at Capernaum or as He delivered a sermon on a hillside nearby. Mary chose to leave her home, including a life of arranged marriage and the security of extended family, to follow Jesus and His band of twelve. Her choice was probably a radical move that necessitated abandonment of her father's family as well as former religious customs. Mary will stay with Jesus until the end and bear the news of His resurrection to the others.

The women at the tomb "report to the eleven and to the rest of the apostles all the things they had seen," and this will transform the small body of believers (John 24:10–11). Why were three simple women the first to see the angels, hear from the resurrected Christ, and receive a message of God? This group of women, in varying degrees according to their freedom, would have followed Jesus as He traversed the countryside. Despite the fact that Jesus was wanted as a criminal, these women—each named Mary—stayed loyal when they might have been arrested and put to death. Peter's fearful denial in the dark is proof of their great risk.

Moving on to other Marys, Matthew provides an interesting side story about Mary, the mother of Zebedee's sons—James and John. This Mary approaches Jesus with her sons to ask that they sit at His right and left hands in the future kingdom. He explains that to sit at His right and left hand is not "mine to give; instead it belongs to those for whom it has been prepared" (Matthew 20:20–22). Later, this same Mary is found at the foot of the cross, weeping and later bringing spices for Jesus's body against others' warnings and her greatest fears. Mary believed the truth about Jesus's new kingdom of God and accepted His explanation of His unique role and the roles of her sons.

Additionally, the headquarters of the Jerusalem Church was likely at the home that belonged to another brave Mary, the mother of John Mark—a young man who would later become an apostle alongside Paul. John Mark's mother obviously had the financial means to manage such a home, yet interestingly, her husband is not mentioned. We will see this same pattern of women acting alone repeated in the actions of Lydia and Phoebe, Paul's friends and coworkers who each served in a church plant. This Mary is documented as hosting the gathering where Peter arrives after he is miraculously released from prison, where he was taken under orders of the magistrate for speaking about Christ. Followers of Christ are gathered together in an upstairs room praying for Peter, and a servant named Rhoda answers the door when Peter knocks. After commotion and speculation, Peter is urged to come inside where he tells the group about the deliverance of the Spirit (Acts 12:12–17). Mary's boldness is revealed in her brave choice. The church in Mary's home is assumed by scholars to have been the first Christian center in Jerusalem, so much that Peter, as leader of the movement there, would hasten to her home upon his release.

Even a cursory glance through the book of Acts reveals that women played a significant part in the spread of the Word through miracles of the Holy Spirit. The lives of Dorcas (Tabitha), Priscilla, Lydia, and Nympha enliven the ministries of Peter and Paul. In the sixteenth chapter of Romans, Paul mentions Phoebe, Junia, Julia, Tryphena, and the mothers of Rufus and Paul. These women acted as brave apostles alongside strong men. Their lives demonstrate the varying types of devotion and courage that first-century women must have portrayed. The unique ability of women to bear up under duress, cling to a cause, and give birth to new life was as evident then as it is now.

The true process of birthing the church of Jesus required not only courage but also competence and preparation. Just as a young mother prepares herself by learning the rules and methods for birth, groundbreakers of the early church had to be competent in their work, or it would not succeed. If the women who supported Jesus wavered or lead others to the church homes, all followers could be charged with treason. If women who hosted fellowships did not earnestly believe in their cause, learn the Word of God, and teach it with confidence and strength, the message would have died. Only the valiant efforts of people who knew what a beautiful cup they held could manage to carry the church into a new age.

Birthing of anything—a new idea or a unique way to carry on—requires ingenuity. In my own work, I have seen many young mothers work diligently to prepare for the new unknown. Questions are asked, such as "How much can I bear? Who will I choose to help me during this pivotal time? Will this all be worth it?" Many young women approach the process of birth with trepidation and fear.

"You don't know me," said one of my first students—Joni. "I am always afraid of everything. I don't know why I'm even attempting this. People I teach with keep telling me I'll never be able to accomplish a natural birth."

Yet not unlike these brave women who followed Jesus to the cross, Joni emerged from being an apologetic girl, often hiding behind past failures, to a strong young woman who birthed with dignity and joy. We worked together. We pondered fears to overcome in our hearts without having to explain them to others. When a tiny boy was born without medication and intervention, there were tears of joy and a great sense of accomplishment. I saw Joni years later. She had a second child, was principal of an elementary school, and was "clothed with strength and dignity," like the woman of in Proverbs 31.

My Home Is Now
a Church

How did the first church services really begin? Jesus left no instructions for a day at "church," except to "go and make disciples of all the world," baptizing them into fellowship (Matthew 28:19). The fertile soil of the early church was prepared and then cultivated with care, just as a mother takes care of her body when she prepares to have a child. As the book of Acts reveals, the church would grow within various types of homes, from modest dwellings to large porticos and villas. Women served as financial patrons, opening their homes from city to village, as we will explore in subsequent chapters. After meeting the charismatic Peter, Paul, and Timothy, women converts developed a fiery devotion that overcame earlier fears of repercussion. Staying with our metaphor, we can describe an eager and willing young woman of the first century church in terms of a young mom anticipating a new birth. Just as an expectant mother, these women, too, waited with eagerness and joy for something they knew would fill their lives with purpose. Their greatest hope was to be found prepared and serving when Jesus returned.

What would such preparation have looked like in the first century? After His resurrection, Jesus had appeared to the disciples— men and women alike— telling them to wait in Jerusalem for God's promise to come. They banded together, facing the uncertainty that He might not again appear. Luke explains in Acts that after Jesus had "given the disciples many convincing proofs over forty days by speaking about the kingdom of God," he was suddenly taken up in a cloud from the Mount of Olives (Acts 1:3). The people who had listened and believed were then left gazing into heaven, wondering where to gather. After a time, and with sad countenances, the disciples and others returned to Jerusalem, fearing their instruction had ceased. They spent the next days "continually united in prayer, along with the women, and with Mary the mother of Jesus and His brothers" (Acts 1:12–14). Jesus's mother had embraced His message with a transformed sense of urgency, it seems. It had not been long since she had approached Jesus with his brothers and sisters, "setting out to restrain Him and saying, 'He is out of His mind'" (Mark 3:21). Jesus had responded, "Who are my mother and my brothers? They are the ones who do this will of God" (3:33–34). Mary was counting herself one of the chosen.

The church was born in power when Jesus's Spirit returned on Pentecost. With the sound of rushing wind, women and men alike were all filled with the Spirit and began to speak with boldness and confidence of all that Jesus had done. The birth happened in the midst of confusion, chaos, and fear—yet what resulted was to change the world forever for good. Followers who accepted the message and believed were baptized. They banded together as a happy, generous and passionate fellowship—a church of God. Luke says that men and women alike "devoted themselves to the apostles' teaching, to *koinonia*, to breaking of bread and to prayers." They sold possessions and distributed equally to all, sharing everything and "praising God, finding favor with all people" (Acts 2:42–47). Among them were the women who had been loyal followers of Jesus Himself. The new band of believers would become known as "the Way" of Christ.

As mentioned in chapter 1, Mary the mother of John Mark provided the first church base in Jerusalem. In Acts 12, Luke recounts that Peter is imprisoned for speaking about Christ after the Pentecost event. New believers, filled with the Spirit of God, have gathered in prayer at the home of Mary. Peter hears from the angel, "Get up and follow me!" The angel leads Peter outside the city gate, and Peter realizes, "The Lord has rescued me from Herod's grasp and all the Jewish people had expected" (12:11). He proceeds to Mary's house right away, and a servant there recognizes his voice at the door. Mary has offered this first church, a place of refuge.

Thwarting Peter's efforts, however, was a zealous Jewish leader, Saul of Tarsus. Saul, a Pharisee, was passionate for the Jewish law and saw this newly formed group of Christ followers as an assault on tradition and Jewish belief. He spent many of the ensuing months breathing "murderous threats" and chasing those who followed the Way. On the road to Damascus to either kill or make prisoners of those in the Christian sect, Saul was pierced by a vision of the risen Jesus in a blinding light. His understanding of the Jewish Messiah would change forever, and his fervor would supercharge the already fertile ground of a fledgling church.

Just as women had supported the ministry of Jesus, women would now house, shelter, and teach for Paul and his apostolic cause. Following the example of Mary Magdalene and those who supported the Christ, women would now become apostles and leaders of early Christianity. The two woman mentioned in Acts, Priscilla and Lydia, alongside other women whom Paul refers to in his subsequent letters contributed in a meaningful, pivotal way to the growth of the church. Each would change the reputation and standing of women in the Roman world. The system of cultural patronage, supporting itinerant teachers and tradesmen, paved the way for women to enter the world of financial support and hospitality. By welcoming followers of the Way into their homes and offering their courtyards as places of worship, such women provided an ark that carried the church through a storm.

Saul, who is soon renamed with the Greek *Paul,* will travel into Galatia, Psidia, Macedonia, and to the coast of Greece to reach the Gentiles Jesus had commissioned him to seek. Many Greek and Latin followers—men, women, and slaves— join the Way of Christ. In Paul's doctrinal letter to the church at Rome, Paul mentions three women who are outstanding among the others— Phoebe, Priscilla, and Junia. In other letters (1 Corinthians and Colossians) and in the historical book of Acts, Chloe, Nympha, and Claudia will be named and praised. Alongside Mary Magdalene, the first of our seven brave women, these six formerly unknown converts care for many apostles called by God. In each subsequent chapter, we will explore women of the Pauline missionary world and their role in patronage and church planting. Each woman lived a dramatically different life that would soon be on display. In living their callings, these women would change and motivate the world and readers for centuries to come.

Female Apostles—
Midwives for the Gospel

One of my favorite birth memories is the night when I met my friend Hope at the hospital. Hope was on her third baby, but she was still eager to have a natural birth and intentionally stayed away from the hospital until she was close to delivery. We met at 11:00 p.m. outside the emergency room. Hope walked slowly to the door holding her back, and her husband carried her bag and pillow, walking ahead of us both. He stood an unusually long time at the door while I stopped with Hope to talk her through a contraction or two. When we got to the sliding glass, a woman in scrubs stood on the other side and motioned to us to walk around the hospital to the other side so we could get a wheelchair, which was their protocol for a laboring woman.

This was like asking Hope to walk back home. The nurse turned and walked away, and Hope and I stood there staring at each other. Suddenly, Hope started pounding on the glass. When the woman came back, Hope told her that she was about to have this baby, so we needed to get in *now!* The woman left. We sat down in the grass for a minute and knew the baby was not far off. I knew she was capable of birthing in the grass if need be. In a nearby parking lot, a doctor shut his car door and began to head quietly into the doctor's entrance and up some metal stairs. Hope and I quickly climbed the back stairs and followed him in, realizing we might get in some kind of trouble or, even worse, be asked to leave. We hurried to the maternity floor, and baby Lizzie was born quite soon after. Hope was defying the culture of hospital protocol, but there was a greater purpose to her determination. Everything worked out beautifully.

Early Christians who followed the message of Paul the Apostle were constantly under similar pressure, having to make frequently choices to defy the ruling powers. The first three decades of the early church (AD 33–63) consisted of underground teaching, instruction, and preaching. The intent was to spread the Word and spread it quickly and with great force. Jesus would warn His disciples that the kingdom of God was advancing under the will of God and that strong men would try and oppose it. Small home churches and worship fellowships took place under Roman surveillance and often the threat of death. Paul plants a church in one place, stays for several weeks of months, then is often chased out or beaten to the point of exhaustion. He routinely leaves his new church plant to take the message elsewhere, despite rough and rocky journeys each time. Paul's determination and grit helps him to write letters to encourage those who fostered his communities for Christ.

Frequently, Paul refers to the male and female apostles who support and minister within the growing movement. The book of Acts offers a detailed record of many courageous women. Lydia and Priscilla figure into this story in a major way, and Chloe and Nympha are mentioned in the letters of Paul. Nympha, Phoebe, and Tryphena will be prominent names in Romans 16. Acts 16 is a beautiful account of the conversion of Lydia and her subsequent actions as head of her household. A resident of Philippi, a Roman colony and leading city, Lydia likely founded and housed the first church on mainland Europe. Her boldness allows the church to be stable and grow, so much that it is deserving of Paul's letter in 62 AD.

After an escape from jail, Paul returns to this church hub in order to "see and encourage the brothers" before fleeing to Thessalonica and beyond (Acts 16:40). In Corinth, Paul would meet and share residence with a Jewish man named Aquila who had recently settled there with wife Priscilla, since Claudius had ordered the Jews to leave Rome (Acts 18:2). The couple would assist Paul in founding the church at Corinth and then travel with him to Ephesus, making disciples of many. The pair are mentioned as cowriters in Paul's subsequent letter to the Corinthian church, sending their own "warm greetings in the Lord," along with the church that met in their home (1 Corinthians 16:19). It is even assumed by some scholars that Priscilla may have coauthored the book of Hebrews with others believers who did not know Christ, but did know of Timothy and Paul.

Additionally, in his letter to the Corinthian church, Paul mentions a certain Chloe, whose household members have reported to Paul that there is "bitter rivalry" among church members that has caused division (1 Corinthians 11). Chloe is apparently a respected church leader, as much of the content and tone of Paul's Corinthian letter comes from her bitter report of infighting and disunity.

What would the home church have looked like, within the large and bustling cities where they were found? Emperors Nero and Domitian were in power during the crucial first years of the early church and were both great persecutors of Christians (64–68 and 81–82). It was not an easy task to be a follower of Jesus in a time when defying the empire brought torture and death. We must appreciate this imminent danger in order to understand the bravery and strong character required of any Christian follower. The sixteenth chapter of Romans describes and praises three strong women whose efforts uniquely propagated the ministry of Paul amid the dangers of daily life: "I commend to you our sister Phoebe ... she has been a benefactor of many" (Romans 16:1–2). "Greet Prisca, who risked her own neck for my life!" (16:3). "Greet Junia, "my fellow countryman, outstanding among the apostles" (16:7).

As the church gained strength, women would stand out among the leaders of faith. The era of martyrdom was dawning, and women would be counted among the tragic martyrs and heroes, as history well documents. In the midst of opposition, women such as these named above continued to offer their hearts and homes for places of gathering. Without their daring choices, church as we know it today may not have survived. Men were most normally occupied in forums, on the battlefield, or working within the government, so women who ran house churches slowly redirected historic Roman attitudes toward females.

According to Carolyn Osiek, early Christianity's hidden churches actually worked in favor of Christian expansion and offered an alternative route for a Roman woman. Such a woman might discard her old belief systems and absent husband to join the Christian faith and house church movement. Suddenly, she was valued and needed, and there was a place to find fellowship. Christianity spread this way quickly, family by family. Despite the fact that under Roman rule, the early church was deemed illegal and often persecuted, the numbers of Christians amazingly grew. We will return to the historical setting of the early house church and the crucial patronage of Christian women in coming chapters (Osiek and MacDonald 2006, 155).

The early church began to develop customs that cemented it tightly. A reference to a Christian "love feast" is found in an apocryphal manuscript known as *The Passion of Perpetua and Felicitas*. This well-crafted story tells of the imprisonment, trial, and execution of two Christian women martyred in North Africa in 203 AD. According to the story, the women, having partaken of their last ceremonial meal of bread and wine, were celebrating "not a banquet, but a love feast!" They turn to the mob and warn them of God's judgment, stressing the joy they anticipate in suffering for the cause of Christ

(Mursurillo, 1972,125). This "love feast" embraced the cup of Christ's suffering and celebrated the community breaking of bread. Such gatherings came to be known over time as the Eucharist— Greek *eukharistia*, meaning "thankfulness." Emperor Nero passed shocking edicts allowing centurions to kill Christians for not bowing down to Caesar, much like Nebuchadnezzar had done in the days of Daniel. Christians who refused to bow were thrown into the arena or burned as torches in the streets.

The simple act of sharing in the cup of Christ would embolden believers and give them courage to faithfully walk to their inevitable deaths.

How did members of the church stay loyal in such attacks? For safety, people gathered inside homes, where sacred worship took place, such as reading of scripture and sharing the communal cup. The sharing of stories and tales of courage encouraged followers to band together in common purpose. As sponsors and hosts of these early home churches, courageous women were vital support. Inside their humble dwellings, or outside in painted and tiled courtyards – prayer groups, worship, teaching, and even labor and birth were known to occur. Laughter, tears, conversions, and rich story-telling nurtured many.

Eventually, the founding apostles spread. Peter eventually settled in Caesurea and later in Rome. Paul worked with both Jew and Greek to plant churches in Macedonia, Philippi, Corinth and Ephesus. He would be martyred in Rome between AD 64–65, only adding fervor to the Christians left behind. Worship communities formed in spite of the watchful eyes of Roman officers. Each of these early practices became commonplace and soon emerged as part of what it meant to be a "church."

As we explore the female Pauline apostles, we can discover how they bravely carried the church like a mother carries a child until it can walk on its own. Equipped with the type of love and support a mother is designed to bear, these mothers of the early church would house and care for their own.

Lydia: Who Was She?
Who Am I?

Imagine yourself a single woman in the first century, sitting by a river to find solace. Life can be a demanding test since Roman guards patrol everything and watch for any who would defy the emperor and his control. You mean to do well, but you're tired of keeping up with the noble women of beauty and wearing expensive gowns with gold brocade. Today, you want to rest. You deal in cloth, as one of the few avenues open to women, and purple cloth travels in wealthy circles. Your home is one of the large *domus*-style dwellings occupied by wealthy freedmen during the imperial era. Your fine home has inlaid marble paneling, doorjambs, and columns, and it is enlivened by paintings and frescoes. You go most places—to the forum, the games, the marketplace—alone, without a husband by your side, since your husband is a Roman centurion, or a favorite of Caesar, or absent for some simple reason you do not understand. Maybe someday he will come home.

This season of life you have found yourself with adolescent

children who are tended by tutors, a large Roman home to tend to, and an equally large household to help with cooking, working and cleaning the inlaid tile and stone. Today, you have taken a few servants and a man at arms to protect your group. There is a small place of worship on a hillside by a stream, and maybe you will find some peace in worshipping Hestia, the virgin Greek goddess of the hearth and home. *If I pray to Hesita*, you think, *she will fulfill me with domestic hopes, more family, and a calm sense of order in my Roman world. She is my hope.*

The air is crisp and dry since you live in a hilltop village. It is early spring, and flowers have not come forth, but tall, lime-green grasses rustle in the wind. You enjoy walking beside the cooling stream. Your pale blue gown is dirty on the edges, but that is no problem for your household crew who work dawn to dusk to keep your linen clean. You smile because today is special, somehow. Husband away or no husband to be found, you are a woman of influence on your own. Your name is Lydia.

Lydia, founder of the first church in Europe, yet a woman who had no idea her name would be part of history. What was Roman society like for Lydia herself? In antiquity, women were traditionally seen as second class, but rules were slowly changing under the authority of progressive Rome. The ancient Pythagorean letters, a collection from fourth century BC to second century AD, were written in part by philosopher women: Theano, wife of Pythagoras, Myia her daughter, and Perictione, the mother of Plato. These well-written letters state that while the main occupation of woman was to manage her house, a wife and husband also "shared other duties and roles, along with the prized qualities of courage, justice, and temperance." Hellenistic women living around 60 AD such as Lydia could also assume the larger role of household manager—the *materfamilias*— if the husband had gone to war or was deceased. They began to enjoy a great amount of freedom under the later Caesars. This may have been the case with Lydia, and the reason she came to the water that day to meet Paul (Bednarz 2002).

According to Carolyn Osiek, Greek/Roman society may not have been as rigid as we have assumed. Although a conservative male perspective is often quoted in literature, historical research shows an interesting reversal: Hellenistic and Roman documents depicting "household management" call the wife "mistress of the household" and in control of all things family and of household affairs (Osiek and MacDonald 2006, 157). Lydia was head of her own household. "A dealer in purple cloth from the city of Thyatira," she has an established trade of her own (Acts 16:14). Thyatira was a town in central Asia, not far from Ephesus. It is one of the seven churches mentioned in Revelation and, as such, was part of John's warning and instruction from the Spirit of God (Revelation 1:11). The seven towns of John's eschatology showed the different realities of church life, both good and bad. Such a place of prominence in latter writing indicates that eventually the message of Christ found its way to Lydia's hometown. She may have had a role in such transmission (Osiek and MacDonald 2006, 159).

The "purple cloth" that Lydia sold had important uses in the Roman empire. Purple—known as Roman Tyrian purple—was the color of royalty and likely invented in the city of Tyre in the first century AD. A color somewhere between blue-violet and red-purple, royal purple was made from a species of whelk, a soft sea creature that lived in a colorful shell. It is likely that Lydia designed and dyed her own fabric, with the dyeing portion of her business located in her home. Such a business would need to be situated near a river due to the need for water and waste material. Although dyes were not chemical, permanent staining could occur. Lydia's neighbors would have wanted her to be at a distance from the community, as dyeing fabrics with powders and toxic liquids omitted a certain amount of stench (Hirst 2017). Luke suggests in Acts 16 that Lydia has her own household, who all agreed to be converted at her command. The Greek word οικοκυριό comes from *oiko* (house) and *kurio* (Lord). The story says that "The Lord opened [Lydia's] heart to listen eagerly to what was said by Paul," so the lord of the household (Lydia) turned the hearts of her staff. She and her household are baptized, and she urges the missionaries to come and stay at her home. Such communal conversion is rare in the Pauline letters. Another instance of this group conversion takes place when Paul and Silas are imprisoned in Philippi after healing the tormented slave girl. When an earthquake releases their bonds, the quaking jailer asks to be saved. Paul tells him to only believe, and that he and "his whole household will be saved" (Acts 16:31). In addition, Paul remembers that he baptized the household of the guard Stephanus when he writes to the Corinthian church (1 Corinthians 1:16).

Historically, Philippi was an outpost a short distance away from the bustling Greek city of Thessaloniki. At the time, Philippi was a Roman colony and "leading city of the district of Macedonia" (Acts 16:12). Founded by Philip II of Macedon, father of Alexander the Great, Philippi was for years a center of struggle between Greece and Rome. When Paul and his missionary coworkers arrive in the late 40s AD, Philippi has fifteen thousand residents, multiple religious cults, and a plethora of military veterans with nothing to do. Insurrection is easily quelled. Philippi is close to the port city of Neopolis, where Paul would have entered from Asia and the Aegean. Trade and travel worked their way through Macedonia by way of a wide Roman road. Today, a visitor can stand in the ancient village of Philippi on pavers from the seven-hundred-mile-long Via Egnatia that connected the eastern city of Byzantium to the Adriatic coast. From the vantage point of small Philippi, it was true that "all roads led to Rome" (Longnecker and Still, 2014 196).

Romans had various types of cults, including the prominent cult of the emperors. For Paul to preach an ideology of a crucified but exalted Savior and Lord, calling Jesus the "Son of God" would not have been welcome. Caesar himself had co-opted the name "son of a god," so defiance was risky. Lydia's quick belief and baptism were very brave. Even Paul found more people who would receive him away from the Jewish synagogue and out among a gathering of women at a place where they went to pray to their gods, or to the foreign God of the Jews. Luke tells us that the woman named Lydia, "who worshipped God, was listening" (Acts 16:14). The Lord allowed her heart to be open to Paul's persuasive message, and she paid attention and believed.

Lydia's next move was to invite Paul and his companions to consider her home as a welcome lodging. Paul and Silas accept hospitality at Lydia's insistence for a lengthy period—enough that her house becomes a central hub for preaching, teaching, and evangelism. When Paul and his co-workers encounter difficulty with the law over a slave girl they have healed, they quickly "enter into the house of Lydia with all the brothers and sisters. When they had seen the brethren, they encouraged them and departed," Luke says (Acts 16:40).

Knowing all of the background to Philippi and the setting of her world, imagine yourself again as Lydia again. You are a Roman businesswoman who has an important trade and the respect of many, having authority over a large household that takes care of your needs and your home. You have heard about the God of the Jews and have listened at the markets or maybe in the synagogue itself. You awaken on the Sabbath day, and something says to you, *Go to the river's edge and pray. Go where it will be safe and pleasant, and you will find Me.* So you follow.

At the river, you see three men washing and laughing together. *Why would people be laughing? There is so much unrest, so much pain in the world,* you think. A small, muscular man approaches you and asks your name. He saw you quietly staring at the riverbank and twirling a dry reed in the water. He noticed your countenance and almond-shaped green eyes. "Where is your husband? Why are you alone here?"

You tell the man, "My husband is gone for long periods of time. I don't know where he is." You pause and look down, feeling the wind blow your hair just from its gold comb. "I have a good trade, though! I create purple cloth, the color of the emperor. My husband is not interested in my work, but he does support me with money for my trade."

"What can I do for you?" the man asks. "What are you looking for here?"

"I am praying to the God of the Jews, hoping He will grant me some happiness and peace," you reply. "I have a wealthy life, by many standards, yet I feel empty and often alone. I have a good job, but I feel my life has no real meaning. Why is that? I pray to the God of the Jews, but He seems very far away."

The rough, tanned man shifts on the rock and looks away. *What must he think of me?* you ask yourself. *He must wonder what's wrong, why I would speak to him this way, or why I'm even here. And why am I here after all? What's missing for me? I have a nice house, a husband, a household, a place in society. I have everything.*

The man turns and looks at your face. His eyes are brown, and yours are a beautiful green, as you are of Roman descent. He stares into yours. "I have the answer to your heart," he says. "I know a man who lived, taught, and died and rose again to prove to us that life is not all about what we see or what we fear. I can tell you all about this man who is part of the one true God Himself. I can explain to you how He can save your hopes and dreams, and make your life complete."

You think, *This is too good to be true! Can I trust this Jewish man?* "What must I do to be saved by this holy man, this man of God?" you ask. "What sacrifices does He require of us? Can He help me find purpose and hope, even if He is already gone?"

The rough man explains all things about this Jesus to you, and He helps open your mind to understand the Hebrew scriptures. He explains how this Jesus fulfilled the Law and the message of the ancient prophets. He gives you hope about a deeper purpose in life, beyond a respected trade or the adulation of many, this insignificant, laughing man you have never seen before. You believe him. You call the friends in your household; suddenly, you see them differently! *They are my friends, my neighbors, my equals!*

The man calls to his friends to come and join you. *We are all alike,* you think. *We are one.*

Riverbank at site of ancient Philippi in Eastern Macedonia.
Paul may have met Lydia beside this river.

Ancient mountaintop Eastern Orthodox
monastery in Meteora, Central Greece.

Byzantine church, Athens.

Church marking site of ancient Philippi in Eastern Macedonia.

Priscilla—Teacher, Leader, Brave Friend

Over time, Rome had become a city on lockdown because of the fear and pride of the ruling class. Emperors Claudius and Nero were gravely afraid of the new Christian sect, dreading its following and its tacit challenge to the divinity of Caesar. They were threatened by the increasing strength of the Jews as well. By 64 AD, much of Rome had burned down, and Nero blamed the Christians. When we first meet Priscilla in the eighteenth chapter of Acts, she is an exile from Rome, her beloved hometown. She will return there one day to minister about "the Way" of Jesus, but for now she lives in Corinth. Priscilla and Aquila arrived in Corinth around 49 AD, when Emperor Claudius first expelled the Jews from Rome due to "incessant rioting at the instigation of someone called Chrestos," according to a Greek Historian. Jewish Christ followers who added to the number of new Chrestianoi in Rome were blamed for the discord and told to leave (Longnecker and Still, 2014 172).

When Claudius died in 54 AD, both Greek and Jewish Christians would return to their communities in Rome.

Priscilla is a Jew, along with her husband, Aquila. Both were probably taught the Way of Jesus from men and women who spread throughout the empire after the diaspora from Jerusalem itself. It is possible that their Jewish-Christian community in Rome traced its roots to the event of Pentecost, when pilgrims visited Jerusalem and became followers of Christ due to the Spirit of God. Acts 2:10 includes "Visitors from Rome" as part of the participants in the events of that day. Jewish Christian communities had formed all over the Roman Empire, and Paul would work to bring the Gentiles into fellowship with first generation Christians who had known Jesus.

Why is Priscilla mentioned so many times as working alongside Paul? The news of God's living kingdom, offering forgiveness and grace, has grasped her heart, and she is full of this Good News of Christ. Her past is forgotten, and she is empowered by a loving spirit who shows her how to teach and train other believers in Christ. Priscilla is mightily convinced that this is the way to follow the God she has always worshipped. We know from Acts and 2 Timothy that Priscilla becomes a teacher who instructs others about the man Jesus—one who came to teach about the kingdom of God, was crucified by the Romans, and then was resurrected into heaven with Yahweh. Priscilla will eventually travel to Ephesus with Paul and there teach "the Way of Jesus" to traveling Greeks, Syrians and Jews. We first find her with her husband in Corinth, however, where the two are tentmakers, and this is how Paul discovers them. As Christians, they must have felt alone in a busy, cosmopolitan, and cultured world.

As confused as Priscilla might have been, Corinth will prove to be her training ground for working in the church. Like Priscilla, our own difficult realities often turn out to be preparing us for something new.

Imagine that you can see life through Priscilla's eyes. You sit in the shade of a rock outcropping and work with thick, heavy needles that weave in and out of goats' hair cloth. You learned tent making from your Jewish parents, and it is a stable, necessary trade. There is an exhausting aspect to the long days of tanning, sewing, and laying the flaps out to dry. Thankfully, the rougher parts of the work are always done by your husband. The marketplace is busy, as Corinth is a bustling city of urban trade and a seaport with more than its share of wild and rowdy life. People come for a number of needs: to trade in bronze or fine metals, to shop for animal skins or other cloths, and to meet at the civic *bema* or "judgment seat." There are public baths in Corinth and even public toilets of stone that operate using networks of water ducts. Most importantly, however, people come to worship at the many temples and statues. Prevalent gods Apollo, Asclepius, Athena, Demeter, Serapis, and others are commonly worshipped with money and sexual offerings. Corinth, in fact, is known as a "shining jewel in the crown of Roman imperial order" and replete with pro-Roman practices and sentiment (Longnecker and Still, 2014, 175).

You are more than aware of these facts. *Who am I to try and speak to these Greek people who are nothing like me?* you muse. *What if we are wrong in our worship, and we are discovered?*

Your husband, Aquila, comes to the small shop you keep inside the rock outcropping. He wanders inside the cool cave-like setting and looks for tools he cannot seem to find. Leather tanning tools, smooth stones, and jars of liquid line the makeshift shelves.

"Are you tired, Priscilla?"

"I am always tired." You look up from where you sit to see the commanding Temple of Apollo under the skyline of the majestic Acrocorinth. It towers over the city like a banyan shade tree. "Why are we here, Lord?"

Aquila's hoarse voice again. "We are alone in this city. We need some help in our home if we want our brothers and sister to gather there as a worship place. What will the children learn on the streets? I wish we had not come."

"They can learn the trade," you respond. "We will stay as long as God allows. Only He knows what will happen next. We must believe."

Days pass. Visitors come and go. It is hot, dry, empty of Jewish practice and law. *What purpose can God possibly have in us being here?* One day a silent, ragged man walks up to you and extends his hand. He is smiling in a sincere and humble way. He looks kind, intelligent. "I am a tentmaker. Can I join you?"

This new friend named Paul is skilled in your trade. A native of Cilicia, Paul is many miles from home, but this is commonplace. People travel throughout the Empire to find work and comfort, to explore the known world. Paul's home province sells a good grade of goats' hair, the primary material for tents. The exported hide is called "Cicilian cloth," and you know it well. Over time, you see he is quite skilled, and you recognize that his parents practiced and taught him the trade. You talk. You share stories of the God of the Jews and then tales of how He has brought you there. At first, there is fear. *Do we speak about our faith in Jesus?* This man is unusual, passionate, humble, and unashamed. He asks if he can tell you the marvelous news about his Jesus, his Christ. You are delighted to share that you already know Him.

Paul asks to join the Way and to worship in your home. You accept, of course. He wants to hear your story: "How did you encounter the Spirit of God? Where did you first learn about Christ?" Paul shares his remarkable meeting with the Lord on the road, a light so bright it landed him flat. He is changed. Paul is a skilled teacher, you soon learn. There will be hours under the silvery olive trees, date palms, and craggy laurel trees learning the message of Christ, learning to speak of the truth and be bold with those you teach. At times, you will laugh at the devotion of this man who only knew you recently as "wife of Aquila."

But you, Priscilla, have a special gift, a calling and purpose. You are a teacher and one who can interpret the gospel message boldly for the cause of Christ. You are brave. Paul sees this in you and encourages your curiosity and your gifts. Each Sabbath, he goes to the synagogue and tries to reason with the Jews and Greeks.

You follow, admire, and listen. Paul's devoted friends Silas and Timothy join him. Soon, you will be explaining the message to many, including other followers who have misunderstood or gone astray. You are a leader of a home church in the small apartment where you live. It is tight, but your floors are always clean, and everyone can sit cross-legged while they eat. Your husband always lends support and his household authority, but never hindering you. You will befriend this Paul who wanders among Corinthian homes, "testifying to other Jews that Jesus is the Messiah." The local Jews oppose and insult him, accusing him of blasphemy, but he shakes the dust from himself and confesses, "From this time on, I will go and preach to the Gentiles" (Acts 18:5–6). No one has ever done this, and you are amazed.

Many in Corinth will hear Paul, become believers, and be baptized. Even Crispus, leader of the synagogue, will come to believe, along with his household. You long to be part of this great movement of God, and are astounded by its power. Other groups of angry Jewish men will rise up against Paul, even dragging him before the governor at the *bema*, the stone heart of the city. You stand and watch this valiant man confess, admit that he is indeed persuading people to worship God in new ways.

"Paul, you are bold! Please tell me where I can find this boldness," you ask.

The man with the dark eyes looks at you and says, "Come away with us—both you and Aquila. I need the passion you have to teach the Way. I need Aquila's steady hand. Join us, and I will teach you even greater things about the One we follow. Come with us; we will sail to Syria, and I must travel on from there." And so you go.

Brave Priscilla. You board a ship that takes you far away from home, and as you rock and land upon the waves, you wonder, *What am I doing now? I have truly left everything now.* You will follow in Paul's footsteps in Ephesus, teaching and training, even preaching in the home church you will start. You will never lose Paul's companionship until the day he waits alone in a dark prison in Rome. Even there, you will visit and be encouraged:

"Paul, tell me how you are. Our Roman ministry grows! We are many in number now. Here is some food—some bread, figs, and sheep's milk cheese. It is small, but the Roman converts have sent what they can."

"I am happy, as I know am loved by you and many others," Paul will reply. "I thank my God every time I remember you and Aquila and the believers in Corinth, Ephesus, and Rome. I pray to our God that you are always bold witnesses for the Lord Jesus in our city, as I know you are. How is your teaching, your family?"

"We are okay now, but life is hard," you respond. "Guards roam the streets and eye us with distaste, as we look like the Jews we are from birth! They continue to blame things on us here, and we are afraid of showing our faith. Our home church continues in different places, and we are happy when we meet to pray, to eat together, and to share the Feast. We love to tell the story about how you spoke until late in the night in Ephesus and the young man Eutychus fell from the window! Everyone loves to hear how you stretched out over his body and brought breath again to his body."

"Ah, I am pleased," Paul says as he sits back against the wet stone wall. "The Lord is moving among us and will be with us forever. And you, Priscilla, you are my brave friend."

Let's visit Priscilla as she progressively appears in the Bible text. In Acts 18:1–3, Paul has left Athens and gone to Corinth; he meets a Jew from Pontus named Aquila who recently arrived from Italy with his wife, Priscilla, or Prisca, as Paul will pen her. After a time of trial in Corinth, the three leave for Syria and land in the port of Ephesus. Paul, or possibly Aquila, has shaved his head in Cenchreae in keeping with a Nazarite vow. Such a vow often included making an offering of one's hair, which would have been offered in Ephesus by one or both men (Holman Christian Standard Bible 2010, 1899). Paul leaves the others behind to depart for Antioch, as he foretold, yet he promises to return and visit the churches (Acts 18:18–19).

Priscilla and Aquila manage to set up a new Ephesian church in a believer's home, using tools they learned in Corinth. In the process of setting up worship, they meet a Jew named Apollos who has arrived from Alexandria, Egypt. He has been "taught the way of the Lord" by missionaries who arrived in Egypt after Pentecost. Although enthusiastic, Apollos knows only of John's baptism of repentance and faith. Prisca knows what to do and remembers the clarity and centrality of the beautiful story taught by Paul. She stops Apollos one day after his brief speech in the synagogue and takes hold of his cloak.

"Please, sir, you are very learned in the ways of our Father God," she may have begun, risking Apollos's criticism since she is only a woman. "You knew of the Baptizer?"

"Yes," Apollo replies. "He baptized many in the waters of the Jordan. Repentance and belief in God are our new calling as Jews! We must lament and wail, listen to the prophets and begin a new devotion to Yahweh."

"Oh, but that's just what we are teaching too," says Prisca. "We believe in the new walk with God, but there is so much more to the story; it doesn't end with confession and repentance. This man Jesus came to show us the way of life. He, too, was baptized by John, but he proclaimed a new kind of kingdom, one that is coming right now through the Spirit of God. Jesus died at the hands of Rome, but he was raised to a new life, eternal life by our Lord."

Prisca invites Apollos to the humble place where she and Aquila have made a home. She and her husband carefully explain the way of God more accurately, and Apollos becomes a new disciple.

Exploring the possible lives of female leaders can help us understand who these women were, and in so doing we can appreciate our own lives and callings. Building on their scant biblical descriptions, some poetic imagination helps a reader to reconstruct Prisca's life. Priscilla's continues to appear in Paul's ministry, and her influence, for example, is described by not only in Acts, but by Paul in his letters to the Corinthian church that were written from Ephesus. In Paul's undisputed letters, evidence for her ministry is found in his letter to the church at Corinth, written in AD 56. Paul closes with familiar, encouraging words: "The churches of Asia greet you. Aquila and Priscilla greet you warmly in the Lord, along with the church that meets in their home. All the brothers greet you. May you greet one another with a holy kiss!"

In his letter to the Roman church, written in AD 57 from Corinth once again, Paul asks the Romans, "Give my greetings to Prisca and Aquila, my coworkers in Christ, who risked their necks for my life. All the Gentile churches thank them" (Rom 16:3–4). Their teaching and influence were far flung.

In Paul's pastoral letter to Timothy, Priscilla is also noted. Timothy is the loyal young disciple who acts as Paul's emissary to the Philippian and Ephesian churches. Paul's letters to Timothy were probably written during the beginning of the patristic era (62–64 AD) and part of the larger effort to organize coherent church structure and framework for leadership. Some debate whether they were written by Paul or by leaders within his Pauline legacy, since Paul was under prison guard in Rome for several years. Nonetheless, they are addressed to Timothy, who is working in Ephesus and dealing with false teaching. In 2 Timothy 4:19, Priscilla is mentioned as a partner of Paul, and her contributions are known to be significant. "Greet Priscilla and Aquila," requests Paul, "and the church in their home; send greetings to the household of Onesiphorus." This certain Onesiphorus was a believer who ministered to Paul during his Roman imprisonment, "searching for, and refreshing [Paul], unafraid of his chains" (2 Timothy 1:16). This mention alongside Priscilla seems to indicate he might have been one she pulled away from false behavior and teaching (HCSB 2010, 2095). Again, we see her significant ability and impact.

The missionary couple of Priscilla and Aquila has "one of the most complete surviving migration histories of any other individual partnerships of similar status" (Osiek and MacDonald 2006, 215). The two workers reveal the distances it was possible for migrants to travel back and forth across the Aegean and the wide range of contacts they could make. Priscilla and Aquila were each uniquely gifted to carry the word of God. Their hospitality, teaching, and leadership became invaluable supports for Paul, so much so that he could leave them in an area to run the ministry there. Hospitality was a respected virtue, both in Roman life and in early Christianity. Priscilla would have been at the forefront in the hospitality of this pair, and we can learn from her intentional practice. Oddly, yet not by accident, her name is always cited first when Paul writes about the missionary couple. This indicates not only her importance, but a subtle upending of traditional hierarchies. Christianity was indeed a revolutionary system in many ways.

In setting up home churches, Priscilla and her husband would face many challenges. First, they would have to find work in the town, earn the trust of clients, and find a suitable place to comfortably settle and stay. Such physical obstacles were common for itinerant artisans traveling the Roman empire, yet each step took time. Paul would fit this category as well, being obligated to construct a living situation and tenable livelihood for himself each place he visited. We can assume that, in both Corinth and Ephesus, the couple found work as tentmakers, and when back in Rome again, they would have to do the same. Each place of ministry would represent a new start and new set of challenges. Life was not an easy road for simple craftsmen.

Once back in Rome, Priscilla and Aquila would have become known immediately by the fledgling church in hiding. As Paul seems to indicate in his letter, the "readers and hearers" would have known exactly how to find them. The city of Rome had different levels of housing, including rooms in an inn, lodging houses, or guesthouses for those of greater means. Artisans might look for shanties or huts outside the marketplaces, or missionaries like

Priscilla and Aquila might have stayed with Greek Christian brothers or fellow converted Jews. Some of these arrangements would have been supported by donations from wealthy Romans or from patronage, which we will explore in the chapter on Phoebe. We know these details because Luke describes a situation in Rome: "The Greek brothers and sisters in Rome heard we [Luke and Paul] were coming, and they met us at the Forum on the Appian Way. Soon other brothers joined us at the Three Taverns. Paul was encouraged and thanked God!" (Acts 28:14–15).

Luke describes many times the way that Paul and others were housed and supported. In their journey from Syracuse in Sicily to Rhegium and onto Puteoli, Paul and Luke "found believers and stayed with them seven days" (28:13–14). Previously in Tyre and Sidon, the coworkers "found some disciples and stayed seven days." Upon departure, says Luke, "All of them with wives and children escorted us out of the city to say good-bye" (21:4–6). When Paul and his companions arrived in Ptolemais, they "entered the house of Philip the Evangelist and stayed with him there" (Acts 21:8). Patronage and support were vital to the spread of Christianity.

Only a few married couples overall are mentioned in the work and ministry of Paul. Priscilla (also called Prisca) and Aquila are Paul's dear friends, Andronicus and Junia are noted in Romans 16 as "outstanding among the apostles" (specifically Junia), and Philogus and Julia are mentioned as partners in the gospel's spread. Scholars term these couples "missionary partners." Sometimes, they were married, and other times they were joined together for protection and influence. For many reasons, ancient missionary arrangements were not based on the systems in place for missionaries today, and many assumptions we make about mission work are based on our modern understanding. Paul refers to this in 1 Corinthians 7:32–34: "I want you to serve without concerns. An unmarried man is concerned about things of the Lord—how he can please the Lord. But a married man is concerned about things of the world—how he may please his wife—and his interests are divided." The same is true for his instructions to unmarried women (Osiek and MacDonald 2006, 227).

Paul seems to give the same instruction to all women who are in service to the Lord. While we cannot be certain about ancient ministry situations, it is likely these couples were married since the marriage relationship and its effects on life under God's law were significant to the Pauline mission. His messages about husbands and wives and the importance of loyalty convey his belief in covenants and other commitments held by early Christians. Priscilla and Aquila would surely have been part of Paul's example of married life as God intended.

Priscilla's role shows us a history of real women in the first century and how a woman could make her own place given ingenuity and devotion to the Christian cause. Bible translations have often shaped women's identities to suit purposes of male audiences and authors. Given this reality of ancient culture, the roles of women in leadership were often downplayed. Ironically, the Christian message was written (largely by Paul) to validate both prominent women and women of humble circumstance. In so doing, both types of roles within the empire might gain importance and legitimacy. According to Rodney Stark in his 1996 work, *The Rise of Christianity,* women outnumbered men in early Christian circles and enjoyed higher status there as compared to Greco-Roman society. Their various "social networks" contributed to expansion of their beliefs, and the common marriages of Christian women to pagans had a dramatic ability to affect church growth (Osiek and MacDonald 2006, 223).

Throughout the New Testament, Christianity is described by Luke, Paul, and Peter, and later by other Pauline school authors, to be an orderly religion worthy of recognition and praise. Over time, it would gain respect within the empire's priorities, resulting in the fifth century declaration of Christianity as an empire-wide practice. Both Priscilla and Lydia are described as women of independence and value, and they are recognized as major contributors to the founding of the early church and even to the writing of its history. According to Harold Attridge, scholars have proposed that Priscilla may have coauthored the letter to the Hebrews. Early readers such as Origen, he states, recognized that the style of Hebrews differs from that of Paul's undisputed letters. Often seen as a "letter of exhortation," Hebrews was likely written after 65 AD to encourage Christians to look to God alone through the work of Christ (Attridge 2006, 2035). Priscilla's influence is felt still today, and her determined boldness can challenge us to find our own areas of contribution and where to leave our own unique marks on Christian history.

6

Phoebe—Patron, Deacon, Valiant Emissary

I commend to you our sister Phoebe, a servant of the church in Cenchrea. I ask you to receive her in the Lord in a way worthy of the saints and to give her help as she may need, for she has been a great help to many people, including me.

—Romans 16:12

Once, I had a childbirth student named Shannon who showed up on my doorstep with a suitcase. Shannon wanted to keep her baby, even though she was unmarried, but others in her family weren't keen on that. She needed help. Shannon lived with me for nine months, and during that time, she helped me with my children, spent time learning about childbirth, and sat on my porch reflecting on what had gotten her to this point in her life. She was a small girl, and sometimes, I rocked her as she sat on my lap in a chair. Over the course of months, Shannon decided she was okay without her parents' approval and wanted to have a strong birth with dignity.

We spent many hours preparing. We read the Bible and prayed. In the end, she did have a beautiful birth and married the baby's father soon after. She was determined and strong, carrying all we learned together into her life. Shannon wanted to pattern her life after mine, so she ended up having four more children by way of natural birth. Although this young woman started out small and afraid, through love, prayer, and dignity, she became brave.

When I think of Shannon now, I am reminded of Paul writing to the Corinthian church to compose first a letter of instruction, but also one of goodwill and love. "Do we need a letter of recommendation from you? No, you yourself are my letter, written on my heart, recognized and read by everyone. You are Christ's letter, not written with ink but with the Spirit," he insists (2 Corinthians 3:2–3). The changed lives of the Corinthian people, along with their determination and faith were evidence enough for Paul. He needed no other proof that God was real and active than the believers' transformation. Shannon was that kind of evidence for me, and continues to be so today. She is a person who carries my "letter" forward in life.

Phoebe may have represented just this same follower for Paul. We meet Phobe when she is part of the entourage of believers in the area of Corinth. Her hometown Cenchreae was just east of the large city center. We know Paul spent time in this village, because Luke states it was there that Paul "shaved his head because he had taken a Nazarite vow" before leaving for Ephesus with Priscilla and Aquila (Act 18:18). Today, Cenchrae is gone, but the ruins of Corinth show that people from surrounding cities came down to its city center from the hills to trade, shop and worship there. Phoebe is known for supporting apostles by the common method of patronage, which included acting as a financial patron to the itinerant messengers of Christ. It is implied she was a prominent Roman woman who held the respect of many within the Cenchreae church community. Prominent citizens in the Greco-Roman world not only had wealth, but they were noted for spending it for the public good. Paul recognizes this in Romans 16:

> I commend to you our sister Phoebe, a servant (G.
> διάκονος, deacon) of the church in Cenchreae. I ask you
> to receive her in the Lord in a way worthy of the saints
> and to give her any help she may need from you, for she
> has been a great help to many people, including me. (16:8)

Why does Paul speak of Phoebe as a single woman, not as part of a missionary team? How did she get such renown?

According to Paul's account in Romans 16, Phoebe is one of several apostles who displayed evidence of a woman conducting work for the sake of the gospel with no one by her side. Paul's use of wording, calling her "our sister, Phoebe—our αδελφή (adelphe)" could refer to female member of a missionary partnership alongside Christian brothers, or to a woman acting alone (Osiek and MacDonald 2006, 215). Other single women whom Paul will mention in Romans 16 are an unspecified Mary, partners Tryphaena and Tryphosa, Julia, Junia, and Persis. Paul is careful to cite each person with a greeting that somehow commemorates her service and role: "Greet Mary, who has worked very hard for you" (Romans 16:6); "Greet Tryphaena and Tryphosa, those women who have worked hard in the Lord. And greet my dear friend Persis, another woman who has worked very hard in the Lord" (16:12). Due to the feminine endings, it is assumed they are all female. Other women are mentioned along with their male counterparts: "Greet Andronicus and Junia (whose name was changed in translation for many years to "Junius"), my fellow countrymen and fellow prisoners" (16:7). "Greet Rufus, and also his mother, and mine ... Greet Philologus and Julia ... Greet Nereus and his sister ... and all the saints who with them" (16:15). What is the setting for Phoebe, and why is she mentioned in Paul's letter? Paul is writing to the Roman church from his home in Corinth around 62 AD, on one of his later visits there. As stated above, he likely met Phoebe during his first visit when he worked with Priscilla. Phoebe may have had several roles in the Pauline mission. As a Roman woman, she may have supported Paul with patronage, or she could have offered her home to serve as a house church. Phoebe may have subsequently traveled to Rome bearing Paul's letter, as she may have been heading there for business purposes of her own. A number of scenarios could explain her involvement as an emissary. Paul had firm intentions to spread the gospel to Spain, and Phoebe may have been part of his future traveling team. According to Osiek, an official envoy bearing a letter was to "be received in the same way as the sender would be received, as the authoritative representative of the one sending." Phoebe would have functioned this way with regard to Paul, just as Timothy and Titus served as bearers of Paul's letters and acted as personal overseers in his church communities (Osiek and MacDonald 2006, 215).

Phoebe is referred to as "benefactor of many." She must have used her money wisely for the benefit of many Christians, not just Paul. Paul is somehow in debt to her "sphere of influence in order to expand his mission in Cenchreae." He sees her as an equal coworker, able to bear his epistolary work to another city entirely. Offering to be a host for house meetings or hosting traveling Christians, Phoebe may have helped to introduce Paul to other benefactors, and in his letters, he uses several titles and descriptive adjectives that seem to indicate this, such as "sister," "deacon," "minister," and "servant" (Osiek and MacDonald 2006, 228). As will be discussed below, such were the various meanings of διάκονος in the first century and beyond.

For various situational reasons, Hellenistic women were often acknowledged as household managers—the *materfamilias,* as compared to a *paterfamilias* of the family. One might assume this of Phoebe since her name is mentioned alone, without a man's before or after. In many ways, Greek/Roman society was not as patriarchal as we have assumed. Although a more conservative male perspective is frequently represented in the letters of Paul, historical research includes Hellenistic treatises that describe "household management" with a wife as mistress of the household and able to make her own decisions, travel plans, and choices. Other Greco-Roman writers give similar pieces of advice: "Υυναίκες (*Gynexis*—Women), do not chasten your slaves, or run the household by maintaining discipline like a stringed instrument, not tuned too loose or too tight," and give payment appropriately, when it is due. Such ancient advice was commonly known to be addressed to females as managers of their own households. Women are the presumed authority over its resources, and were expected to administer those resources wisely (Osiek and MacDonald 2006, 149–151).

Additionally, the idealized Roman *matrona* was one who "not only maintained her virtue, but also spun and wave cloth for clothing the household." (Remember our study of the role of Lydia as a "dealer in purple cloth" in chapter 3.) Slowly. the expectation that women would manage their households crept into Christian literature, as cited by Paul in his letter to Timothy: "Therefore, I want younger women to marry, have children, and *manage their own households,* and give the adversary no reason to accuse us!" (1 Timothy 5:14). In his letter to Titus, Paul instructs older women instruct younger women, to love their husbands, and "to be good household managers" (*oikourgous)* (Titus 2:4–5). Later Christian writers followed the same themes of women as administrators. John Chrysostom writes, "A wife takes care of all tasks a man cannot undertake easily, even if determined to try ten thousand times." The repeated theme in Christian and other literature says that despite the veneer of male supervision, the household was really a "system run by women, a woman's space" (Osiek and MacDonald 2006, 152).

Phoebe is described as both a benefactor and "deacon of the church at Cenchreae" (Romans 16:1). Deacon—G. διάκονος—describes her role within the church, but that function is not totally clear. Deacon was a church leadership role at the time of the writing of Romans, but not a recognized rank. Often the word *diakonos* is translated as minister, servant or helper. Paul even uses the *diakonos* to describe himself and his co-workers. In 1 Timothy 3:8–13, he states as instruction for structure and governance: "Deacons must be serious, not double tongued, not greedy or indulging in much wine. Must hold fast to the mystery of faith." The term for *wives* (γυναίκα) was also frequently translated as "women" (γυνή) and vice versa, so the meaning of women here could either mean women deacons, or wives of deacons.

Was Phoebe a female deacon, given the responsibilities and rights of males in Roman society? Paul continues his church instruction, saying, "Deacons must be married once and manage their children and households well" (1 Timothy 3:10). Due to Paul's mention of women managing the household, this instruction could have been heard for women deacons only, or for men as custom would suggest. Rules for deacons would have been understood by Paul's first readers to be for the ministers themselves and not just the wives of deacons. Paul is not discussing only gender roles in this passage. He would likely not give certain qualifications for just deacons' wives. In addition, the subject of the overall passage is church offices, not marital partners (Aquilina 2014, 28). Phoebe, by inference, would have been a deacon in her own right, and not referred to as a "deaconess."

The role of deacon was to become a recognized term of church structure. The office would become a leadership role without the context of a hierarchal rank. In 2 Corinthians 6:3, Paul describes the noble role of a διάκονος, including his own role as servant, deacon, and minister of the gospel. The role included subservience and support, along with faith in God's message:

> As servants of God, we commend ourselves in every way— through great endurance, in afflictions, hardships, calamities, imprisonments, labors, sleepless nights, and hunger. We are known by purity, knowledge, patience, kindness, holiness of spirit, genuine love, truthful speech and the power of God, and are equipped with the weapons of righteousness. We are sorrowful yet always rejoicing, poor yet making many rich, as having nothing, yet possessing everything. (3–10)

Phoebe, a servant, deacon, and friend to Paul would bravely cross the Adriatic Sea to make the rough and arduous journey to Italy. Not unlike Viola in Shakespeare's *Twelfth Night,* she may have been blown offshore by the fierce Meltimi winds of the Greek isles and run aground for a number of days and nights. In a similar way to the renowned Shakespeare play, travelers' names might be exchanged and identities confused until Phoebe was safely on shore. Arriving at either the port city of Rhegium on the southern toe or the town of Brundisium on the eastern heel of Italy, she will feel herself a foreigner to their Roman culture. It would be hot and dusty, and Phoebe would have to make her way out of the seafaring town with longshoremen and roughnecks walking the shoreline. There is Greek influence in the port towns, but Brundisium is primarily a Roman fishing and trade center. Travelers come from all ports east and south, and the roads would appear confusing at best.

Hoping to cross the boot north to Rome by caravan or camel, Phoebe will be unable to speak the dialects and will have to ask where to go: "How far must I travel on this Appian Way to reach Three Taverns, or the Forum at Appius?"

"The distance is one hundred twenty *mille passus,*" a Roman solider will reply. The journey will take you three days.

It is a long and bumpy journey. Sometimes, the other travelers will bother you and ask where your dress was made and by whom. They will admire your golden hair. Nights will be spent on the road or in a small hut of a boarding home. You will have little to eat, only figs and olives and nut spread on toast. You ask yourself, *Why did I do this for Paul? Will I survive this strange journey?*

Finally, you reach Rome. Weary, you stumble through the alleys and routes that lie in the shadow of the great colosseum. You will carefully ask a few kind looking passers-by if they have heard of the Christian community that forms the hidden church at Rome. Many will look at you as if you have brought a ghost into their midst; they will clutch their burlap bags and move away.

"Woman, *nomen gentile*?" they will often turn to you and ask. "Whose wife are you? Whose daughter? What are you searching for?"

After some time, and maybe several days, you will meet a person who looks kind and knows the answers for your questions. His name is Andronicus. "Yes! I know of the community you seek. We are in the home together on Domani Street, just past the curve of the alley here. We are upstairs and meeting tonight for fellowship and the feast of love. There you will meet Tryphaena and Tryphosa, Junia and our dear friend Persis who has just recently joined us. We will have bread, wine, olives, and meats. Dinner first, and then the feast for our Lord."

You are overjoyed. At long last! Breathless, you say to him, "I have the letter from Paul, the letter where he explains to you our righteousness in the Lord!" Andronicus smiles sincerely. This man is most anxious to hear how all of you from Corinth are faring and how the church is growing there. "I am Phoebe," you proclaim. "Our beloved brother Paul has written much of great value for our learning in the faith here. He speaks about our joy in believing, and how we must live as those who are righteous before the Lord God. He sends greetings to many of you, to all the brothers and sisters here in the church in Rome."

"We are so ready to receive encouragement and to hear from our beloved apostle," Andronicus responds. "We are many now, a large band, and we are ready to face whatever Caesar brings—persecution or ridicule. We can do all things through the Spirit of Christ who strengthens us, like a mighty wind in our bones."

With your clothing tattered and your hair astray and unkempt, you make your way with this kind man to a set of narrow stone stairs. Climbing up with his help, you greet the family with kisses and smiles. Groups from all quarters of the city of Rome are there, and you are amazed at their numbers. They are all worshipping as one *ekklesia*, one assembly and body. Soon you are asked to eat the noonday meal, break bread for a common feast, and share the news of your church at Cenchreae. You begin to read for the men and women spread out on the dirt floor, surrounded by children and slaves, full of love for God and His purpose:

> To all who are in the church at Rome, loved by God, called as saints. Grace to you and peace from God our Father and the Lord Jesus Christ. I thank my God for all of you because the news of your faith is being reported in all the world … I want very much to see you, so I can impart some spiritual gift to strengthen you, that is, to be mutually encouraged by each other's faith, both yours and mine … I am obligated both to Greeks and barbarians, both to the wise and the foolish; so I am eager to preach the good news to you also who are in Rome. (Romans 1:7–12)

7

Who Was Chloe, and Who Are "My" People?

Now I urge you, brothers, in the name of our Lord Jesus
Christ, that all of you agree in what you say and that there
be no divisions among you. … As it has been reported to
me by Chloe's people that there are quarrels and disunity
among you, my brothers and sisters.

—1 Corinthians 1:10–11

To revisit the chronology: Paul is writing to the church at
Corinth from far-off Ephesus, where he is staying for a time
before heading back to Achaia to visit his fledgling fellowships
there. The 1 Corinthians letter was written about 54 BC to the large
and prosperous urban center of Corinth. Their diverse population
of international travelers and citizens included people from Africa,
Asia, and Europe as well as Greece. It is not surprising that Paul's
letter was written to address disunity and discord! Some translations
of Corinthians refer to Chloe's "people" who came to notify Paul as
"members of Chloe's household." Why would these people have gone

by ship across the Aegean and all the way to Ephesus to meet with Paul about a church conflict? It is likely that such conflict was a crisis that threatened to damage the reputation of the Christian church at large. How would Chloe's people have been immediately known and recognized, even in Ephesus? Who was Chloe?

Women like Chloe, a central part of the believing fellowships in Rome, had begun to open their houses for gatherings by extending benefits to leaders and apostles like Paul. As stated above, this became well known across the empire as "Christian patronage." According to Carolyn Osiek, "deference, respect, and submission were owed to the patronal figure who was either hosting in a home church, or head of the household in some way by commanding attention and honor" (Osiek and MacDonald 2006, 214). Often the key missionaries known as "founding apostles" were present in the home church. When they were teaching or leading the Eucharist, or Feast as it was called, they received center stage. Just as we saw with Lydia, women who were heads of households are well recorded in the Roman Empire history and termed the *materfamilias*. Such women were often prosperous in business and many times living on their own, surrounded by servants and family. Chloe was one of these women; her reach would have included relatives, slaves, former slaves, and children. Chloe may have been unmarried—either widowed or divorced—or married with an unbelieving husband. Part of her ministry as a Christian home-church leader was to support single women or young women still a part of the father's household. Wives of Roman men, or Jewish nationalists who showed up hungry for Paul's new word of hope, would have been immediately received. One can see evidence that these women church hosts existed in Paul's letters: "Give my greetings to our brothers and sisters at Laodicea, and especially to Nympha and the church that meets in her house" (Colossians 4:15). It appears that Nympha is single, or maybe a widow and therefore free to offer her services to the church and to act as a leader. The church mentioned here may have been in her home, or part of a larger community of churches. The proclamation of the Colossians letter might have even occurred in her house, since she is named. One can imagine the unique impact of a letter read in a house ruled by a *materfamilias* here. Near the end of a Pauline epistle that was read aloud, each group who attended would be addressed directly, with the "members who were traditionally subordinate in the house told to submit to the *paterfamilias*—or *materfamilias* in this case—in the Lord" (Osiek and MacDonald 2006, 18–19).

Paul also writes to encourage the wives of unbelievers, "If a woman has a husband who does not believe, and if he is willing to live with her, let her not divorce … Who knows, O wife, whether or not you will save your husband?" (1 Corinthians 7:13, 16). Peter will write to a believing wife who is alone in her faith: "Be submissive and kind to your own husbands; even if some do not obey the word, they may without a word be won by your conduct" (1 Peter 3:1–2). Household churches, in fact, may have provided cover for Roman women to attend Christian assemblies and convert. In a public setting, such behavior would have otherwise been impossible.

Both married and unmarried women performed patronage roles, often independent of their husbands. We learn this through the stories of Lydia and Phoebe. "To step into a Roman house church was to step into a woman's world," claims Carolyn Osiek in *A Woman's Place* (15). It is not unreasonable to assume that a Christian *materfamilias* who acted as patron might herself be married to an unbelieving husband, in which case she would have to host groups without his support. Roman husbands were often away at war, involved in the Isthmian games, or occupied with aspirations to city governance. An unbelieving, disinterested husband may also have given the believing wife an opportunity to live more freely for the cause (Aquilina 2014, 29). Ironically, such a woman became even more "in charge" in the household and of the children's education and religious training. She could exercise her spiritual gifts of leadership and teaching without his involvement. Her name as *materfamilias* would began to fit intimately and support her various talents and strengths.

Back to the case of Chloe— the inclusion of "her people" might have indicated a large household and even children or husbands who followed their mothers or wives. Paul's immediate recognition of Chloe must indicate she was a central person in some kind of home church network. Her "people" are the attendees at her home, followers of Jesus who supported the centralized Corinthian church. They would have acted as surrogate teachers, messengers, missionaries, and in many cases even midwives for women who came to Chloe's home to worship and observe the Feast (Osiek and MacDonald 2006, 215). It is obvious from historical records that the centralized home church was a welcoming place, even offering room for childbirth and family needs. Alongside this view, some scholars think that Chloe's messengers are writing or traveling from Corinth to Paul on behalf of their own concerns, independent of Chloe. She herself might not be a Christian, since her messengers are referred to only as "her people" and Chloe is not herself in the group. Given such a scenario, Chloe's people may have represented servants in her household who reported to leaders of other remote home churches, even in Ephesus. She might be a believer who stayed home in Corinth with the other members of her *familia,* or she might have been the *materfamilias* of a pagan family. No matter the arrangement, it is clear that Chloe is not a resident of Ephesus, but that her situation is enough to report on. Household members cared enough about the crisis in Corinth to report it to Paul.

According to the rest of Paul's letter, the "disunity" referred to by Chloe's people describes believers who are swearing allegiance to certain named apostles, and not to Jesus Himself. Paul is infuriated by this tendency to make an idol of people bringing the message, and he will make a point in his letter to address this: "I urge you, brothers, in the name of our Lord Jesus Christ, that all of you be united with the same understanding and conviction!" (1 Corinthians 1:12–14). It would have been incumbent upon Chloe to bring such unity to her household.

So the question for us will be, Is it part of our journey to bring unity within our families, households and friend groups? What are some possible answers to the question, "Who are my people?" Looking at the path of a life, it is easy to see that one's "people" are friends and colleagues, neighbors and others within the radar of life experience who need our love, time, and friendship. Our 'people' surround us and take care of us; they stay with us when things are hard, and we vow to stay with them. Our people are those we take care of in many ways. As women, we often have large networks in many different realms. In keeping with Chloe, we can serve and live alongside our 'people' so they will take the time to report to us and others when things are not as they should be.

There are other named women included in the letters of Paul and in the Pastoral Epistles. In the letter to the church in Philippi, Paul encourages Euodia and Syntyche "to agree in the Lord" and not quarrel (Phil 4:2). Not unlike the people who reported from Chloe, these women were reported to have brought the church down with their fighting and discord. They may have quarreled over doctrine, over a man, or over whose home would be the best place for a home church. Paul addresses here in some translations a person named Syzygus, his "true partner" and likely pastor of the church at Philippi. Paul pleads with him, "Help these two women who have contended for the gospel at my side, along with Clement and the rest of my co-workers whose names are written in the book of life" (Philippians 4:3). The term "book of life" is only mentioned in the New Testament in Revelation and speaks of those who are counted among the saved. Paul must have had high regard for the two named women.

Paul also writes to "beloved Apphia, and the church in her house" in Philemon 1:2. Here he is writing from prison in Rome to a certain Philemon, a prosperous businessman living in Colossae, concerning Onesimus, his runaway slave. Paul pleads with Philemon to act in

Christian love and forgive him. Apphia's home would have been the place where Philemon could learn about such love.

Paul greets "Nympha and the church that meets in her home" in ancient Laodicea near Colossae. He asks that his letter to the church be read in her home, which was possibly carried out by Nympha herself. "Pay attention to the ministry you have received in the Lord," Paul instructs, "so you can accomplish it" (Colossians 4:17). He again mentions Onesimus in his greeting, calling him a "dearly loved brother," and implying that he would be welcomed into the fellowship in Nympha's home. Claudia is mentioned as the only coworker in Paul's letter to Timothy: "Timothy, make every effort to come before winter." Writing from Roman imprisonment, Paul adds, "Erastus remained at Corinth, but Pudens, Linus, Claudia, and all the brothers and sisters here (*adelphoi)* greet you" (2 Timothy 4:21). The Greek word used for brothers and sisters, αδελφός, refers here to the Roman believers, both men and women, who were part of God's family (NIV Study Bible, 2011 2099).

As mentioned above, Paul sends greetings in several letters to his beloved "Prisca and Aquila" (Romans 16:3, 1 Corinthians 16:19, 2 Timothy 4:19) and to Phoebe, Mary, Julia, Tryphaena, and his own mother (Romans 16:1, 6, 12, 13). Their role as missionary partners and friends was beyond compare. An interesting detail is that Paul commends a certain Junia alongside her partner Andronicus. Junia's name was changed through the years of translation, as we will explore below, but Mary's and Phoebe's names remained unchanged. Scholars have drawn few definite conclusions as to why this discrepancy exists.

In a unique historical book entitled *Junia, the Lost Apostle,* author Rena Peterson explores what might have been the truth about Junia as a founder of the early church and why her name was changed. According to Pederson, patriarchal rules under the institutional church governed many of the names listed in the New Testament. Newer reference works and commentary on the Bible confirm that the name Junia had once been written and recognized as the name of a female apostle in the early church. Later, church leaders became uncomfortable with a woman apostle and teacher and changed her name to the masculine version—Junius. Over time, Junia's name and acknowledged role were slowly changed. The name of Junia has now been rediscovered by scholars who painstakingly referred back to the early Greek texts in order to resurrect the person herself (Pederson 2006, 2–3).

"Greet Andronicus and Junia," writes Paul, "who were kinsmen and of note among the apostles; they were in Christ long before me" (Romans 16:15). Who was this Junia, whose name was altered to read Junius in ancient papyri and texts? How could she have known Christ "long before" Paul? Junia may have been married to Andronicus, she may have been single, or like Timothy, she may have had a Jewish mother and a Greek father. Paul refers to her as a "kinsman," which could have meant a relative or a fellow Jew. Nonetheless, she learned about Jesus from either a family member or an apostle. She may have been in Jerusalem at Pentecost and witnessed the coming of the Spirit itself. Junia may be a person to whom Paul would also have written, as he did for Timothy: "I clearly recall your sincere faith that first lived in your grandmother and mother … and I am convinced is also in you. Therefore I remind you to keep ablaze the gift of God … for God has not given us a spirit of fear, but one of power, love, and sound judgment" (2 Timothy 1:5–7).

By the way Paul commends her, Junia was obviously a woman of great importance in the early Christian family and a messenger of the Good News. Being an apostle meant that Junia would teach the Jewish law and scriptures to those she encountered along her way. As an emissary of the gospel, she will know the story of Christ and His resurrection to new life by heart. She is one who fully embraced the coming of the Spirit at Pentecost and who continues to live within the power of that day. Imagine yourself as Junia. You will travel the stone-paved Appian Way and the Via Maris to the sea. You will catch boats and caravans, and in so doing, you will ride and talk with fellow travelers who need to know God's truth. God will place you in perfect positions to witness and proclaim His favor. As Junia, you will preach, instruct and care for the flock that Paul has lead you to. You will have fellowship with other believers which will strengthen you for the work ahead. You will create fellowships in the place you call home. Does this describe your life, or something you can one day bring to pass?

The Greek word ἀπόστολος (apostolos) is taken from two words—στέλλειν (stellein)—to send, and ἀπό (apo)—away from. As Junia, you are a person 'sent off' to minister to others. Do you see yourself as this person today? Junia likely travels great distances to visit churches throughout Achaia and Macedonia, returning eventually to Rome and ministering to the church there. She likely passed the great Meteora mountain outcroppings in central Greece, where one day, monasteries will be built atop the hills. In the Agios Stefanos monastery that dates to the fifteenth century, there is a wall painting of Junia that depicts her holding a cross and a book. Today, one can imagine what her life as an apostle may have entailed.

Paul's friend, and possibly relative, Junia commanded his recognition and regard. Junia has been depicted in other paintings and in literature over the years. An inscription on a wall in Corinth from 43 AD reads:

> A woman of highest esteem aided many of our citizens from her means, and welcomed them into her home. In gratitude our people agreed to commend Junia and give testimony of her generosity to our native city and her good will. Our citizens will do everything for the excellence and glory she deserves.

In her story about the life of Junia, Pederson explores the difficulties women may have faced in ancient times to gain respect in the religious world. Even women in the ancient world needed to be reassured that the stories of women mattered. Today, we need to know our stories count, and that we are vital to the history and the ongoing role of ministry through Christ. It has been the purpose of this book to show that our gender matters too, and the stories of our lives are an outgrowth of the strengths that God has given women—to endure, to give birth, and to bravely face life ahead in whatever form it comes. Our gender is, in fact, what can make us strong. Given our role as women who bring life in many forms, we can look forward with hope.

A final birth story comes to mind as we close our story of the women of the early church. It is also a story of courage, and one that began a long friendship with a young mom named Amity. This brave friend continues to inspire me. I met Amity during her first pregnancy, and she was unsure and afraid of attempting a natural birth. I had a large class at the time, and the women soon spoke easily about their fears and concerns. We had a great deal of camaraderie around my living room couch. Amity grew in strength and gave birth beautifully to her daughter, Callie. She took on the mantle of her strength and ability, and soon she had several more children, ending with seven. During this time, she stepped out of her house itself and founded a chapter of La Leche League in our small town, which was no easy task. Amity began to coach other women and assist them in birth. She traveled to learn about aspects of natural birth and taught what she had learned. She grew into a new woman based on her commitment to what she knew God had taught her about babies and motherhood. I was proud to call her my student and friend. Amity is just another brave woman I met out on the road. She is like you.

Saint Lydia of Philippi

Saint Ourania, one of the Virgin Martyrs of Thrace

Saint Phoebe, Deaconess of Corinth

How Do These Stories Apply to Me?

Questions for Group Discussion or Personal Thought

Chapter 1—Three Marys Are Transformed

1. Look at the four Marys listed in the chapter. What do they have in common, besides the name Mary? How can you picture yourself as one of them?
2. What might have happened to Mary Magdalene when she left home to follow Jesus? What continued to draw her to the work of the disciples, and how would her gender make her specially equipped to help?
3. Consider the story of Mary, mother of James and John, who asked Jesus if her sons could sit at His 'right and left hands' (Matthew 20). Mary reappears at the cross. What changed in her heart after she made her request? What must she have rethought in order to come in line with Jesus's teaching?

Chapter 2—My Home ... A Church

1. Imagine what life might have been like after Pentecost. Would you have been willing for people to call you "crazy" for believing God's Spirit had been sent?

2. Following the example of Mary, mother of John Mark, have you ever provided a small church setting for others in your home? What might be an occasion to offer such a thing, and what must change in your life in order to do so?
3. Did Mary's changed heart have to do with her offering home church? What does a changed heart look like for you?

Chapter 3—Female Apostles/Midwives of the Gospel

1. Picture yourself as Priscilla or as the woman Felicitas in the apocryphal story. Could you risk everything for your faith? Could you leave your city?
2. Tell of a time when your courage and belief made you do something bold.
3. What does it look like today to leave things behind and start a new movement of faith, using only the simple tools of your home, your words?

Chapter 4—Lydia: Who was She? Who Am I?

1. How do you see yourself reflected in Lydia's story? Are you a businesswoman with a career? How might you respond to a new call from God?
2. To what can we compare Lydia's 'purple cloth' today? What is it that gives people respect and value in our world?
3. Describe what you think Lydia might have heard in Paul's message that encouraged her to become his friend? Was Paul a credible man?
4. Why would a woman like Lydia, a businessperson of high standing with servants and a comfortable home, have been interested in Paul's message in Philippi?

Chapter 5—Priscilla: Teacher, Leader, Brave Friend

1. Priscilla had a great deal of courage. Do you think she was born this way, or did she learn to have courage from her life experience?
2. What is your particular calling and purpose at this time in your life? Do you think Priscilla's purpose changed over the years when she traveled from Rome to Corinth to Ephesus, and back to Rome?
3. Recalling that Priscilla was a gifted teacher and mentor, we see that her purpose remained the same. If our purpose is lifelong, how does our calling change over the seasons of our life?
4. Priscilla and Lydia were independent women—although one was married to a believer, and one appears to have been alone. Can you still act independently for God, spreading His word, if you are alone in your faith?

Chapter 6—Phoebe: Patron, Deacon, Valiant Emissary

1. Phoebe was an independent Roman woman with means to support others, and possibly a church in her home. How do you support the Christian work you believe in? Can you start something new in that regard?
2. Phoebe traveled over land and sea to take Paul's Roman letter to the church there. What 'journey' are you currently on with your faith? Could you see Phoebe's journey as one that represents any work we do for Christ?
3. Consider Phoebe of Corinth and the fact that Paul asked her to travel with his letter to the Romans. How do you face challenge? Would you have said yes?

1. Given the facts about Chloe as a possible *materfamilias* and host of a home church, can you picture yourself in this same role?

2. Is there an authority figure in your life who you report to about ministry? What does it look like when you are disturbed about people or events under your care, and to whom do you turn?

3. Assuming Jesus calls us to a Christian life of service, what can you do in this season to 'take up your cross' and lead? What did it take for Chloe, a Roman woman, to do so … or for 'her people' to seek out Paul?

Works Cited

Brave Women of the Early Church

Aquilina, Mike. *The Witness of Early Christian Women: Mothers of the Church*. Huntington, Indiana: Our Sunday Visitor Publishing, 2014.

Attridge, Harold W., Ed. *The Harper Collins Study Bible*. Society of Biblical Literature, 2006.

Green, Michael. *Evangelism in the Early Church*. Grand Rapids, MI: Eerdmans Publishing, 2003.

Longnecker, Bruce W and Todd D. Still. *Thinking Through Paul: A Survey of His Life, Letters, and Theology*. Grand Rapids, MI: Zondervan Press, 2014.

Mursurillo, Herbert Anthony, Ed. *The Acts of the Christian Martyrs*. Oxford: Oxford University Press, 1972.

NIV Study Bible. Grand Rapids, MI: Zondervan, 2011.

Osiek, Carolyn and Margaret Y. Macdonald. *A Woman's Place: House Churches in Earliest Christianity*. Minneapolis: Fortress Press, 2006.

Peterson, Eugene. *The Pastor*. New York: Harper One, 2012.

Description and Rationale for
Brave Women of the Early Church

The idea of writing about the early church came to me as I sat in class at seminary. I began to see how women not only had shaped the message of the Bible but also had been instrumental in guarding the fledgling church and flinging it forward into what we know as the "church age." Their bravery and ingenuity were instrumental in what happened to the salvation message of Jesus and later, of Paul.

Added to this developing awareness were my many experiences with women during my tenure as a Doula and midwife. Women are determined, intentional, and brave when faced with challenge. I discovered that these women I knew and assisted were just like the ones who formed the early church. So in my work, I explain the setting of the first century church and the opposition it faced. I then explore seven women in detail, and I plan to present two of them each week in our sessions. The women follow the order of their appearance in the New Testament: Mary Magdalene, Lydia, Priscilla, Chloe, Phoebe, Junia, and Nympha (last three mentioned in Romans). In each case, I tell her story, then compare it to one of my birth stories or make the person come alive in a fictional account.

Outline for *Brave Women*

Introduction: My book concept, my story of motivation for writing the book
Chapter 1: Three Marys are Transformed
Chapter 2: My Home is Now a Church
Chapter 3: Female Apostles—Gospel Midwives
Chapter 4: Lydia—Who was She … Who am I?
Chapter 5: Priscilla—Teacher, Leader, Brave Friend
Chapter 6: Phoebe—Patron, Deacon, Emissary
Chapter 7: Who were Chloe and others named women? Who are My People?
Chapter 8: Questions for Discussion

Printed in the United States
by Baker & Taylor Publisher Services